Why Your Grandma Talks Funny

COMPILED BY *the Anglea daughters*

ILLUSTRATED BY *Bailey Graham*

Copyright © 2020

All rights reserved. No part of this publication may be reproduced, distributed, or transmitted in any form or by any means, including photocopying, recording or other electronic or mechanical methods, without the prior written permission of the publisher, except in the case of brief quotations embodied in critical reviews and certain other noncommercial uses permitted by copyright law.

Disclaimer

This autobiographical book reflects our grandmother's recollections of experiences over time. Some of the events in her life have been shortened. Great care has been taken to present each story as we heard our grandmother share her memories. Please be gracious if you heard her tell a story somewhat differently than we have shared.

Scriptures used in this book are from the Holy Bible, the King James Bible, public domain.

Dedication

This book is lovingly dedicated to Mrs. Joyce (Christner) Anglea. Her selflessness and commitment to rearing her six children for the Lord has no comparison. We owe her a great debt and truly rise up and call her blessed. We love you, Mom!

This book is written in honor of Nelly Magdalena (Bachmann) Christner. Grandma's desire was to have her story in print and title the book, *Why Your Grandma Talks Funny.*
    Here it is, Grandma! We hope it's everything you wanted!
    Grandma's sweet spirit and servant's heart were admired by all who knew her. There will never be a graham cracker fluff, a cinnamon roll or a revel bar quite like the ones Grandma used to make! We are thankful to have called her "*our* Grandma."

Acknowledgments

We would like to thank Luke and Jessica Anglea, Shannon Johnson and Sharon Thomason for their expertise in proofreading. We appreciate their time and effort to make this book grammatically correct.

Carrie Merriott, thank you for designing the graphics inside the book and the cover. We appreciate your fine detail and captivating designs as well as your friendship to all of us.

We would also like to thank Linda Stubblefield for her layout and book design. We are thankful for your help with this special project.

Carolyn Yoder, Artur Bachmann's daughter, relayed to us many stories that her dad had told her while he was living. She was a joy to speak and work with during this project. Thank you, Carolyn!

A big thanks to Amy Bosnyak and her countless times of proofing, editing and guiding us along this book-writing process.

Table of Contents

Preface by Ben Anglea 9

Foreword 11

Map of Bachmann Family Journey 12-13

Chapter One
    Storytime with Grandma 15

Chapter Two
    The Bachmann Homestead .17

Chapter Three
    The First Goodbye 21

Chapter Four
    Coaches and Castles 24

Chapter Five
    Farm Life 27

Chapter Six
    On the Move—Again 31

Chapter Seven
    Chasing Chickens 34

Chapter Eight
    Angels in the Dark 38

Chapter Nine
    More Chewing Gum, Please!....................43

Chapter Ten
    Hope at Last.................................47

Chapter Eleven
    The Long Voyage.............................53

Chapter Twelve
    A New Adventure............................58

Epilogue
    Why Grandma's Story Is Special to Us...............63

My Mother's Trunk 72

About the Authors 76

Is the Lord Your Shepherd?........................78

Refugee Files and Translations.....................81

Preface
by Ben Anglea

When our third daughter was born, my wife, Ashley, wanted to name her Nellie. That was a special name to her because it was my Grandma Christner's name. When we would go visit my grandparents, Grandma Nelly and my wife would sit at Grandma's kitchen table and talk. They would drink coffee together, and Grandma always had something sweet to eat. Grandma had a sweet tooth and made all kinds of German pastries and goodies! She really spoiled us grandkids but not just with sweets. She spoiled us with her love, smile and that twinkle in her eye!

Grandma Nelly was a special lady. As we got older, we loved to hear her talk about her life! If you asked her, Grandma would talk about her life and family; she would talk about how she escaped Germany, came to America and met Grandpa. Hers is an amazing story—one like so many stories of people who lived during the World War II era. Our daughter Nellie is ten years old now, and she loves chapter books!

So, grab a hot chocolate and something sweet, sit at your kitchen table and let Grandma Nelly tell you her story: how she survived World War II, came to the USA by God's providence and allowed God to do something very special with her life. Enjoy this book, but more importantly, let God do something wonderful with your life too!

Foreword

Have you ever talked with someone who sounded different than you? Did you ask them where they were from or why they talked funny? Well, our grandma sounded different, and many times people would ask her, "Why do you talk funny?" Even her own grandkids would ask her this question. For Grandma, it was a simple answer, "Well, I'm from Germany so I talk with a German accent."

But really, we grandkids found out that it was more complex than that. She was a German refugee during World War II and often fled for her life from the Russian army to freedom. Grandma and her family had many hardships. She lived a life much harder than any of us could ever imagine. Going day to day, not knowing what they would eat for breakfast, lunch or dinner; loading up on a train and not knowing where the soldiers were taking them; saying goodbye to their home, their things and their dad and not knowing when they would see him again; braving the cold and fleeing the enemy armies—all of this was Grandma's life.

We are excited to share this story with you and keep her legacy alive for generations!

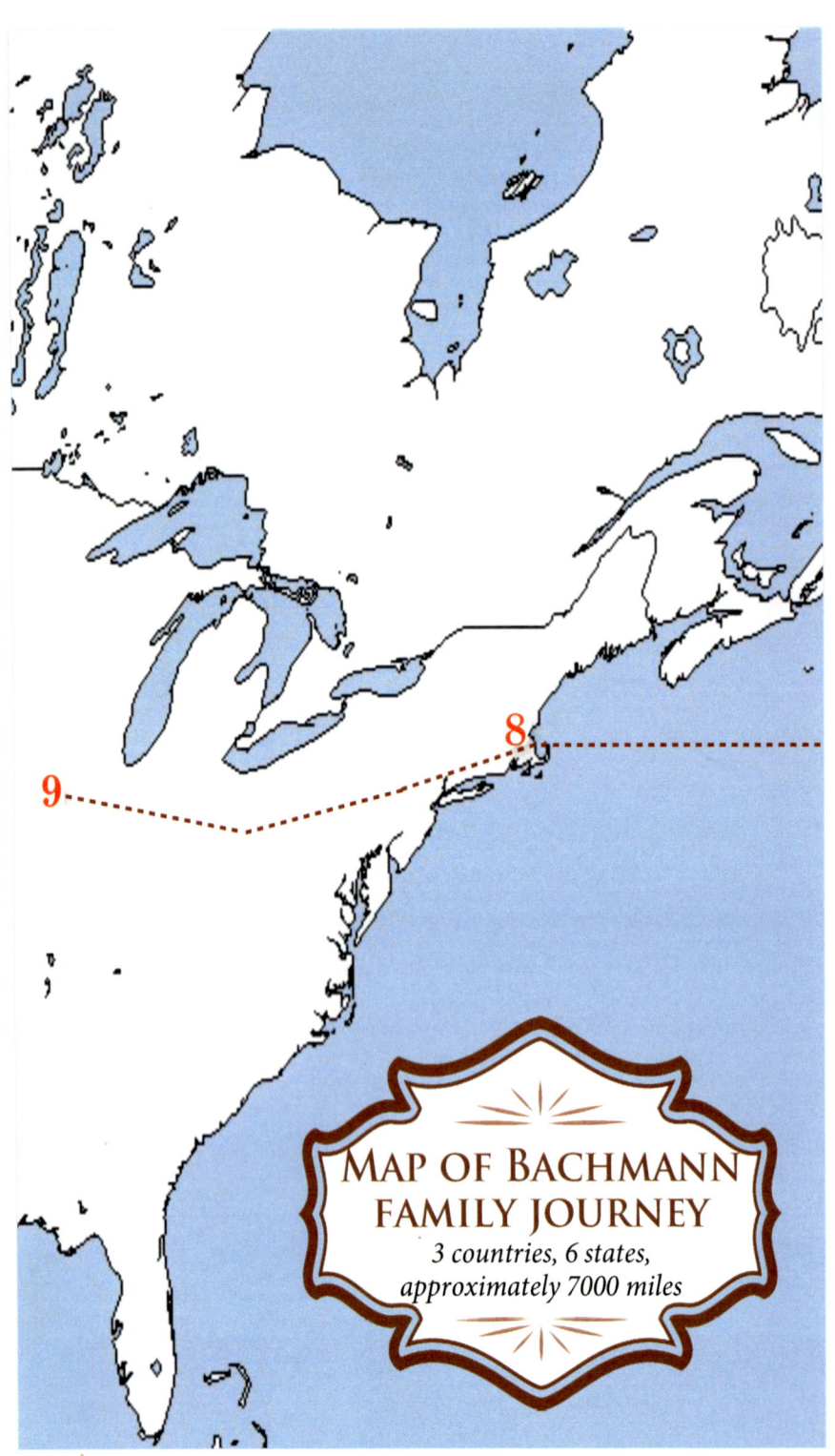

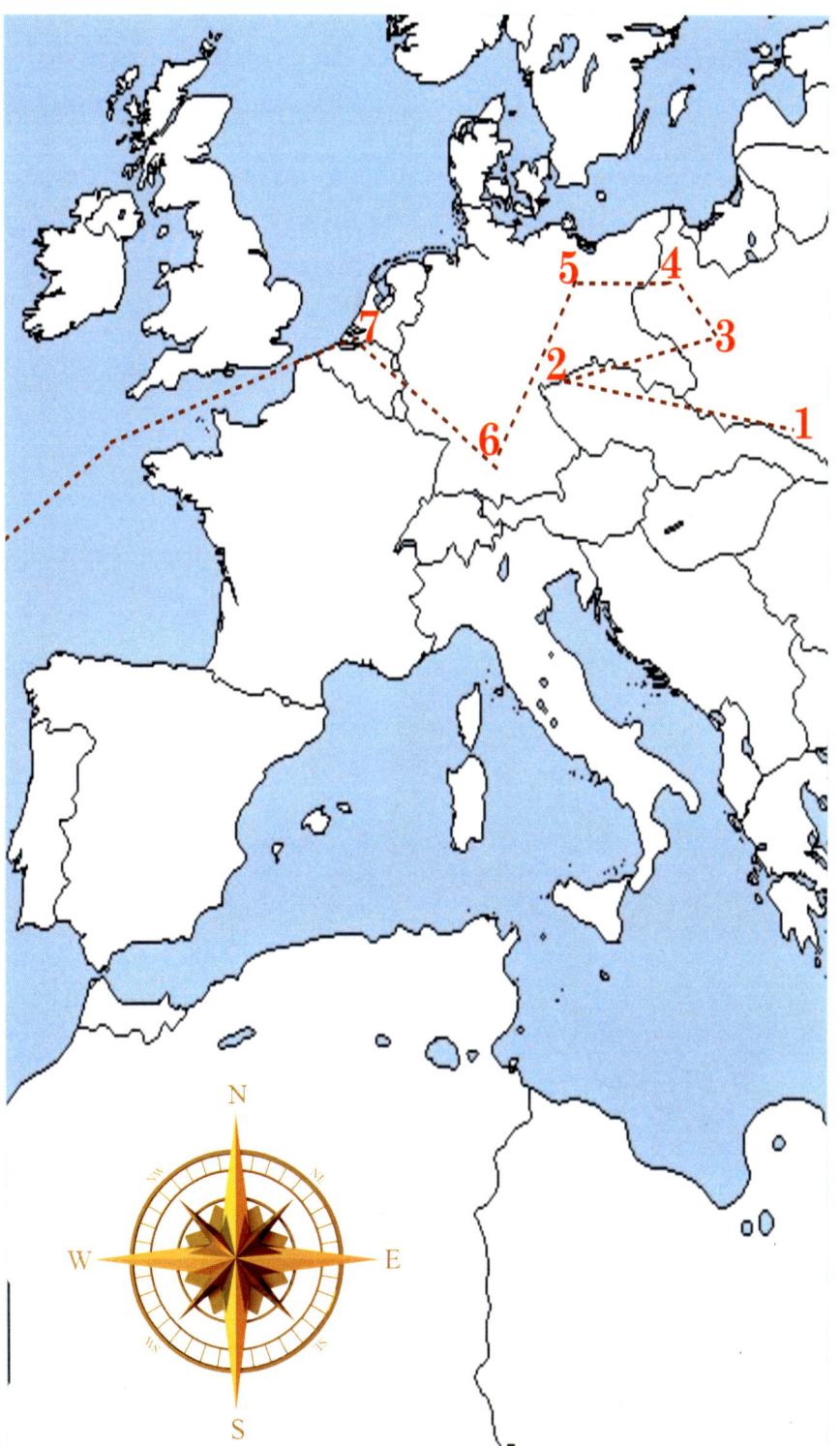

Storytime with Grandma

Kalona, Iowa
1999

"*Trust in the LORD with all thine heart; and lean not unto thine own understanding. In all thy ways acknowledge him, and he shall direct thy paths.*" My mama would whisper this verse to me and my siblings when we would get scared.

This verse means so much more to me now. You see, our path was a dark forest with no glimpse of light. Our horses had strayed from the wagon train, and we had no idea where we were. "How did we get here?" you may ask. Well, my story begins in 1939 in the country of Poland.

At this time, World War II had just begun. On September 1, 1939, Germany attacked Poland; we found ourselves in the middle of a warzone and decided to flee!

CHAPTER 2

The Bachmann Homestead

Falkenstein, Poland
December 1939

*G*uten Tag, my name is Nelly, and I am ten years old. My story begins in Poland. I'm German but we lived in Poland. Germans were great farmers and really made Germany a great agricultural country. Poland, right next to Germany, needed some help with their agriculture so they asked farmers from Germany to move over to Poland and

farm the land. In the 1700s my ancestors were one of the families to leave Germany and farm in Poland.

    I lived in a little house on Lot 18 Falkenstein with my parents, Rudolf and Christine Bachmann, along with my younger brother, Artur, and my baby sister, Mathilde, but we just called her Tillie. Lot 18 has been in the Bachmann family for 155 years. We lived on a farm, but in Europe, we only had one patch of land close to our house. All of the other land my father farmed was spread throughout the village. My village was in a group of seven German villages. There we had a happy life. I remember Father coming into the house every morning from his chores on the farm and saying his prayers while looking out the window.

The Bachmann Homestead

In the middle of our village was a big bell tower and across from the tower, a school and a church. The big bell would ring three times on Sunday morning—once to wake us up, once to tell us to get ready and once to tell us it was time for church. I loved Sundays and remember my father looking out the window praying to God. On Sunday afternoon, my father would sit, read the Bible and pray.

Christmas was my favorite holiday!

"*Vater*, is it time to go to the Timber and cut down the tree?" little Tillie asked Father.

The three of us were so excited to see Father coming in the door carrying a beautiful evergreen tree on his shoulder.

"Hurry, *Mutter*, let's get the decorations out so we can decorate the tree," I said.

Christmas tree decorations were not twinkly lights or beautiful ornaments. Instead, we would decorate the evergreen with candies, tasty decorations, walnuts, wafers and other treats on the thick, prickly branches. On Christmas Eve we went to church and then went to sleep waiting for the *Christkind*—the Christ child angel—to come. In the morning we would eagerly look for the presents under the tree.

"Oh, *Vater*, what a wonderful rocking horse!" Art exclaimed as he sat on the back of a wooden rocking horse with a brown mane and tail made from yarn.

"*Mutter, Mutter,* she is beautiful!" I exclaimed as I held my porcelain doll with her pretty hand-sewn dress. "*Danke!*"

My parents stayed up late most evenings leading up to Christmas to make these wonderful presents for us kids. That was the last Christmas I remember in our lovely, happy German home.

CHAPTER 3

The First Goodbye

*Falkenstein, Poland
to Bad Schandau, Poland
January 1940*

"*M*utter, where are we going? Why do we have to leave our *Vater*? Why are we leaving our little house? It's the only home I have ever known," I questioned.

"*Vater* and the other men will come after us with all the herds. We cannot all fit on the train," Mother tried to reassure us, even though we were not sure when or if we would see our papa again. Even though Mother was nervous about this sudden change, she trusted God to take care of us and unite us all together again.

All of the sudden, my brother, sister and I were loading up into a freight train that was used for cattle. It had no seats, just straw on the floor. It was dark and smelly, like cows or chickens had just been in there. Then two big soldiers came and rolled the door shut and locked it. That's when we got scared because we didn't know if they were taking us east or west. *Where would we end up?* This was wartime, and you never knew what would happen. If they took us east, we would end up in the Russian territory. If they took us west, we would be with other Germans.

The First Goodbye

"We are going to be all right. We are going to trust the Lord, and He's going to take us the right way," said Mother.

After riding in the freight train for several days, with little to eat, we were getting very hungry. Mother always comforted us and helped us stay happy when we were hungry or scared. When we were getting close to the German line, they took us out of the train and put us in a resettlement camp until we could find a new home. These resettlement camps were provided by the Allies of Germany. Thousands of families like mine had to move because the world around us was in turmoil. These resettlement camps became the temporary homes of many people that had to move away from their own homes.

The first thing they had us do at the resettlement camp was go to a big bathhouse and get cleaned up. I guess we smelled after lying in straw for a week! We were puzzled by this bathhouse. It was unlike any we had ever seen. It was a large concrete room. There were long pipes stretched across the ceiling with sprinklers attached to them. I tried to count all of the sprinklers when I showered but gave up at sixty. I bet at least 100 people could shower in there. *But why would they make such a room?* It wasn't until later that we learned the bathhouse was built by Adolf Hitler. He was the Fuhrer of Germany. Being a Fuhrer meant you were not a kind leader, but a ruthless, tyrannical person. He was a very bad man. He used those same showers to execute many Jews in Germany.

Coaches and Castles

*Bad Schandau, Germany
to Gostynin, Germany
Mid-January 1939*

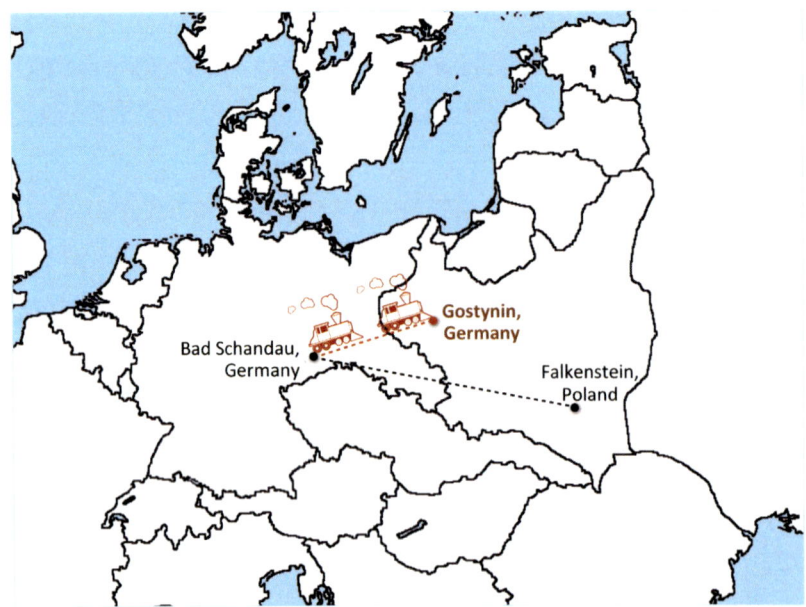

After showering at the resettlement camp, the German soldiers loaded us into a *Donnerbuchse* (in English it means "thunderbox"), which is the nickname for an all-steel train with big wheels. I figured they called it that because the loud rumbling of the coach sounded like thunder crashing in a storm. This train was so noisy, but no one seemed to mind; thankfully, this train had benches. Even though it was cold, it was nice to travel clean this time. I huddled close to my mother to keep warm. Her dark hair smelled a little different than usual, not like the times back home when we snuggled close by the Christmas tree, but I was just grateful to have my red hair clean and fresh again! It had been about two weeks since we said goodbye to our father and left our home.

We traveled for quite a while on that train. We arrived at a train depot and heard the soldiers giving orders to where we would go next. We walked for quite a while, carrying only a small satchel. We turned into the entrance, and Art and I just stared up at the sky in amazement.

"We're living here?" asked Art.

Surely there was some mistake. "Maybe we're living here as servants," I said.

Our new home was a huge castle in Gostynin, Germany. I was kind of excited beginning to think I might have a nice bed to sleep in, but then I looked around at all the refugees with us and my heart sank. We didn't have our own rooms. We didn't even have beds. Our family slept on the floor with only blankets in one corner of a room. There were three other families in our room—one family in each corner. We had good meals because our mothers helped in the kitchen. I enjoyed watching mother peel potatoes with the other women and making such tasty meals.

We lived there several months, and it was so exciting

when spring finally came. All of us children were able to play outside and get some fresh air. We loved to play over by the tower near the entrance of the castle.

Some days were enjoyable and carefree, but some days I could really feel the tension of the war weighing heavily on the mothers. We were living in wartime and you never know what is going to happen in war. My family and I have now lived in two places where very bad things happened to good people because of war. It is hateful and hurtful. Instead of pledging allegiance to the country Germany, the Third Reich was now pledging their allegiance to the leader, Adolf Hitler, and he was wreaking havoc on us and millions of Jews.

Farm Life

Webelsfelde, Poland
June 1940

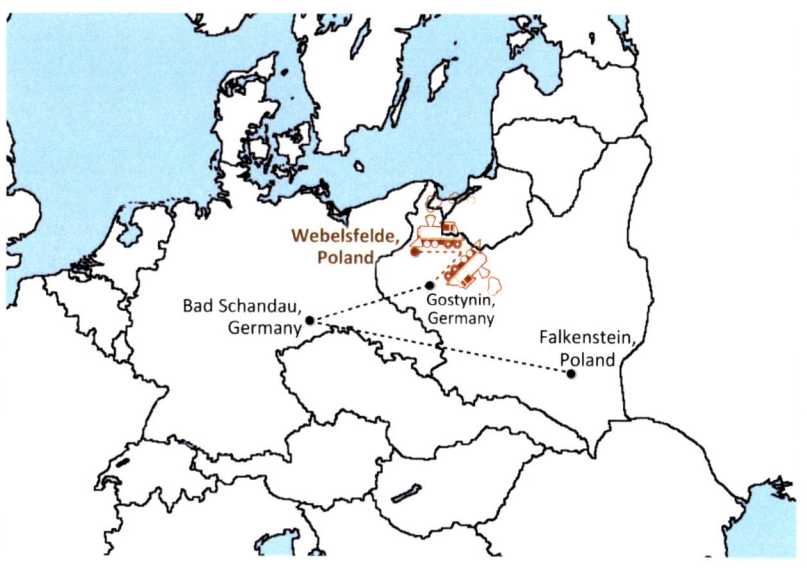

In the spring of 1940, they told us our new home was ready in Webelsfelde, Poland. *How did that make sense? We were just in Poland and had to leave and now we're back in Poland.* Germany had controlled the western part of Poland after 1939, and many Germans were settling there. So, here we were, resettled to a farm in Webelsfelde on the Vistula River.

The fear of war seemed to dissipate with the excitement of seeing our father again! It was such a happy day when we were able to all be together again. We had missed our father so much, and it felt so good to give him a giant bear hug!

We lived on a farm with lots of livestock. It was different from our farm in Eastern Poland. The fields were right around the buildings, and even though it was a village, our neighbors' houses weren't as close to our house as they were in Falkenstein. It wasn't *our* home because another family had started this farm, lived here and worked the land. Just like us, they had to leave their home. It wasn't an ideal situation, but we made the best of it.

During the first three years of living in Webelsfelde, the German army was becoming more forceful. They were still under the dictatorship of Adolf Hitler. By Hitler's command, the soldiers boarded up the local church buildings and used them for grain storage. They did this to take away our religious freedom. Since there was no place to go to church, the families in our town started to meet together in our homes on Sunday. Eventually, that was taken away also. Then they started a program called Hitler Youth Camp for the children and Hitler Union for the adults.

"*Vater*," said Artur, "do I have to wear this silly hat?"

"We can't make a fuss," said Father, "just wear it and when you get home, you can take it right off."

We all wore matching uniforms. I remember Art wear-

Farm Life

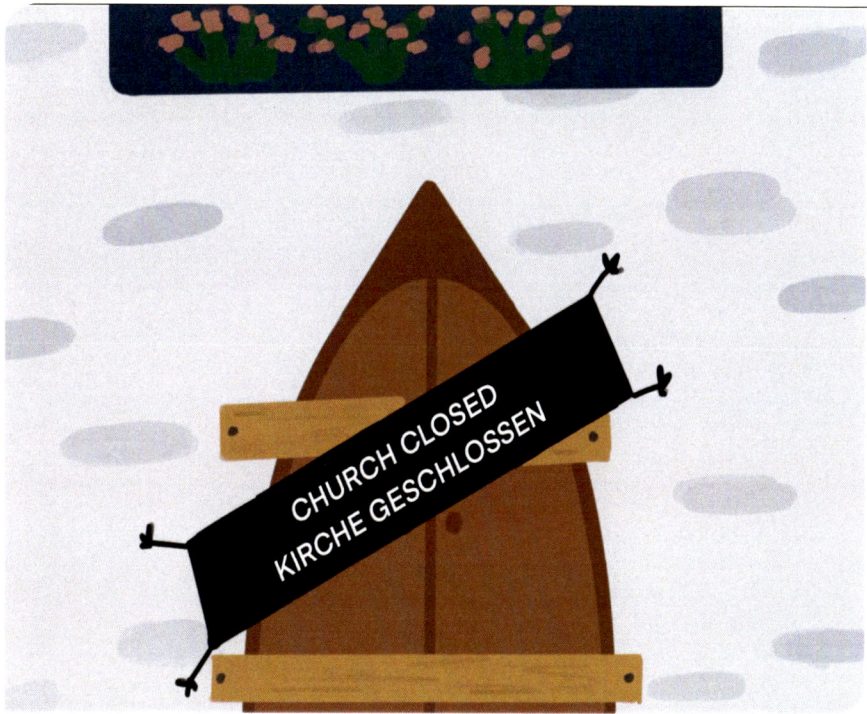

ing tan shorts, a white shirt and matching shoes and socks. Everyone in political authority was being indoctrinated by Adolf Hitler. He was a very bad man, but our group leaders of the Hitler Youth Camp were telling all of us children how wonderful he was and how awful the world would be had he not stepped into power. Not one negative word was heard about Hitler while on the farm. We were forced to believe he was like God, while at the same time, he was murdering millions of Jews in inhumane ways. The castle we just came from was now a concentration camp for some Jewish families. No matter how hard our life was here in Webelsfelde, we were better off than many others under Hitler's rule.

Once again, my parents made the most of our situation. While we were not able to go to church, we were able to attend school. We missed half of the school year traveling last year. It felt so good to be back! We thoroughly enjoyed learning and collecting books on all types of subjects. We lived on this farm for five years; then in 1945, our lives changed again. I was now 15 years old, Artur was 14 and Tillie was 9 years old.

CHAPTER 6

On the Move—Again

Webelsfelde, Poland
January 1945

"The Russians are getting closer, and if you don't want to get caught you have to get away! Get out of here!"

Neighbors came running to our farm with the news. A very nasty battle—the Battle of Stalingrad—had just taken place. The Russians came out victorious and more aggressive than ever. They were advancing into Poland, headed right in our direction.

"*Kinder*, this army is very bad, very mean. If they catch us, they will kill us. We must flee again," Mother and Father explained to us children.

This was a big decision to make. Everything had been pretty calm for the last five years. Now, how do we know for sure that the Russians are getting close?

My parents decided we should leave *again* so they made a wagon out of wood and put a fabric covering over it because it was winter and cold. We had to bring food for the horses so we couldn't bring much food for our family. My mother brought her favorite dishes and plucked feathers from the ducks and geese we raised on our farm. She made us soft blankets stuffed with those feathers, and we put the blankets and dishes in a trunk my father made.

"Can I bring my favorite doll, Mama?" Tillie asked.

"*Ja,* just pick one, dear. We don't have a lot of room on the wagon," she replied.

We loaded up into the wagon and said a tearful goodbye to our father. We didn't know if we would ever see him again. There were several other families that traveled in cov-

On the Move—Again

ered wagons like us. We all followed each other in a single line. It was called a wagon train. We traveled non-stop for a week, stopping only to feed the horses because the Russian army was getting closer.

CHAPTER 7

Chasing Chickens

*Wagon Train
January 1945*

It was a sad time. As I looked around at all the wagons, I saw all the sad and frightened faces. The mothers were acting so brave, but I could tell that it was a very uncertain time for them. My neighbor had three little children so she hired a young girl to go on this trip with them. The girl would help her drive the wagon and take care of the children. It looked as if several other families had done the same.

After a week of traveling, the young girls who helped the mothers decided they should remain in Poland. There was a lot of crying because the women had all the responsibility now—take care of the children, horses *and* drive a wagon in the winter. The mothers were now on their own to lead their families. It was cold, and we were so hungry once again. The only time the wagon train stopped was to feed the horses or eat a little bit of food.

I laid in the cramped wagon with my knees up to my chest. Art, Tillie and I tried to snuggle close under the goose feather blanket all night to keep warm. I peeked out the front

Chasing Chickens

of the wagon at my mother. She held the reins tightly. Her fingers were probably frozen stiff in the bitter cold. She never doubted God. When we would get scared, she would say "*Gott* will do it. *Gott* will take care of us."

One afternoon we stopped to feed the horses, but this wasn't like the other typical stops. This place seemed familiar to me. It was a farm. It looked very similar to ours. Tears welled up in my eyes as I looked around. I couldn't help but think of our farm back in Falkenstein and all the happy memories we made there. I pictured in my mind the happy times when Grandma Bachmann would come to visit along with my aunt. I heard the chickens clucking in their coop nearby, smelled the familiar scent of the

cattle grazing and saw where the harvest of potatoes and cabbage had made for a very fulfilling fall. Whoever lived there must have had to leave everything behind like I had, and my heart felt sad for them.

"*Kinder*, go catch us some chickens so we can have a warm meal," exclaimed the women. The mothers made hot chicken and potato soup. It was so nice to have a meal—and a warm meal at that! It tasted so good, and my belly felt so full! We thought we might get to stay there a few days and sleep on the floor instead of all curled up in the wagon, but once again we heard throughout the wagon train, "If you don't want to get caught, you better go on!"

Some refugees said they were tired and wanted to stay, but Mother said, "I think we better go." Many incidents happened over our travels, but still it was better than if we would have stayed at that abandoned farm. My friend Lily and her family stayed on the farm, got caught by the Russians and put in a camp. Their life was very, very hard because the Russians were mean. God protected my family because my mother was close to Him. He helped her.

One incident happened in a village where we stopped to feed the horses. After resting a little while, it was time to leave, and Art was nowhere to be found. I was so sad because with Art gone, that meant I would have to drive the wagon when Mother needed to sleep. I was so scared, but Mother was calm.

"We will find him. If he doesn't come this time, he will come the next time we stop," she said.

Chasing Chickens

Sure enough, after a little while, we saw an image coming towards us through the fog.

"Here he is!" said Mother. Mother always calmed me.

"Oh, Art!" I exclaimed. "I'm so glad you are here! Mother was getting tired, and I was going to have to drive the wagon—that would have been a disaster! I'm so glad you're here!"

"Me too," said Tillie.

CHAPTER 8

Angels in the Dark

*Wagon Train
January 1945*

Artur took on a very important role at the young age of 14. He was leading our family and was responsible for driving our horses. There were rumors of young German boys being taken from their families in order to join the Third Reich under Adolf Hitler. The German army was now setting up checkpoints at various towns and crossroads. It was now common to be searched and questioned at such places.

I was sitting in the back of the bumpy wagon and could tell our pace had slowed a bit. As we crept along, it became clear that we were stopping. I figured it was another checkpoint, and, sure enough, as I looked out front where Art and Mother were sitting, I could see the German soldiers forcing each wagon to pull over. Our cousin was in the wagon in front of us.

"Artur, I see a path this way. Let's take it to get around the checkpoint," said our cousin.

Art agreed.

Angels in the Dark

As we were making our way, we came upon a muddy ravine. Our cousins and their family in the wagon next to us had a hard time getting across but eventually made it through. We were right next to them, but our horses were sinking into the mud. Their legs were becoming shorter and shorter with each second. Art jumped down out of the wagon to try and help the horses get their legs out of the mud, and Mother just kept saying, "We have to lighten our load! We have to lighten our load!" The obvious items to throw out were our books. The books we had collected the last three years in school and so enjoyed were being tossed out of the wagon into the mud so our horses could pull a lighter wagon. "Quick, Nelly, we don't have time to go through the books, just throw them all out!" exclaimed Mother.

I was hoping that with each book we threw out that the horses would make it, and I would get to keep some of the books we had brought, but alas, Mother was right. There was no time to pick and choose which books were worth saving. With Art down helping the horses and Mother, Tillie and me throwing out our books, we were able to lighten the wagon, and the horses were able to make it through! One thing that stands out in my mind is that our cousins never stopped to help us. That was the sad thing about war. It was every man for himself, and, sadly, that applied to families as well.

"Oh, no! Oh, no! What have I done?" Mother, Tillie and I woke up to Art's voice in the front of the wagon.

"What happened?" asked Mother.

"I don't know. I must've fallen asleep and the horses just stopped! Where's the wagon train?" replied Art.

We could hear the bombs exploding in the near distance.

"Oh, no! Where are we?" I worried.

"I don't know. It's so dark out here," replied Mom.

"Do you see any other wagons?" I asked.

"*Nien,* I can't see anything," Mom said.

It was dark and cloudy. There was no moon or stars. All we could see were the tops of the trees blowing in the night air. We had no idea where we were headed. *Were we going into the enemy line?*

Once again, Mother's calm voice said, "Artur, it will be fine. You are very tired but so brave to drive the horses so I could get some sleep. We will be just fine. The horses are going this way. We will just keep on going." We went on for what seemed like sixty miles. Gunshots in the distance and the hooves of our horses were the only sounds I could hear. It was as if all of us in the wagon were holding our breath for fear of where we could end up. I knew Mother was praying in her heart—praying for safety for our horses, the wagon and for us to get back on the right path. It wasn't long until we saw a light from somewhere.

"Well, God sent us a light!" said Mother.

Angels in the Dark

We followed the light and found our wagon train! What were the chances the light would be from our very own wagon train! We were all so relieved and thankful! There were many times like that when I believe God sent us an angel to help us and guide us because Mom had faith in God.

We traveled for about three weeks like that. All we were trying to do was get across the Oder River just east of Berlin. We had to hurry because the Russians might bomb the bridge, and if we were still on the east side of the Oder River, we would be caught by the Russians.

Once we made it across the bridge and northwest of Berlin, we decided to stop and rest for a bit. It felt so nice to slow down and catch our breath. I could see the tension release from all the mothers' faces in our wagon train. There was a sense of relief amongst the entire group. The horses stayed in one building, and we stayed in the other or under a tree. It was nice to stretch out and sleep instead of curled up in a bumpy wagon.

CHAPTER 9

More Chewing Gum, Please!

Schwerin, Germany
May 7, 1945

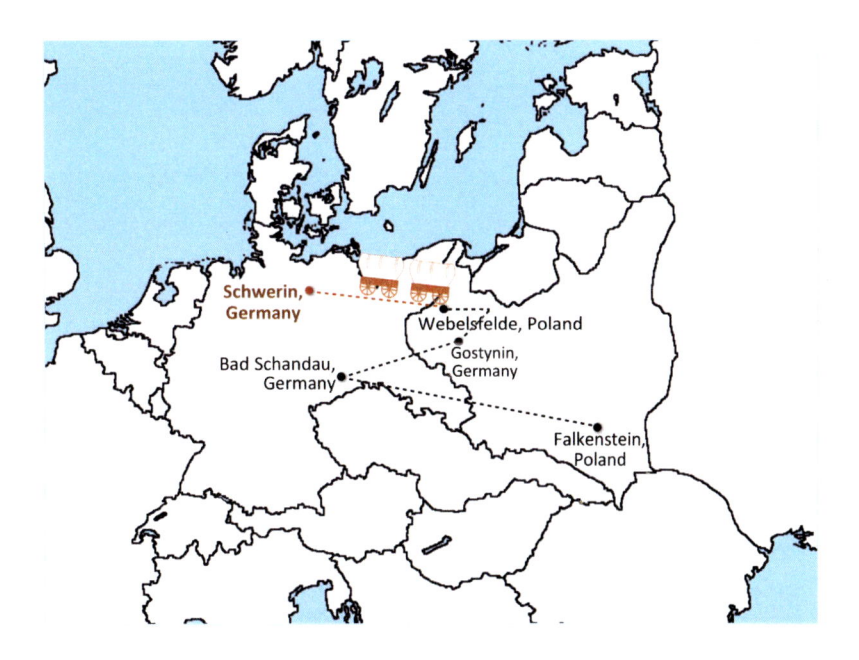

After four months, we heard the most wonderful news! "We don't have to go any farther! The Americans are coming." Armies from the East and West had invaded Germany, and Adolf Hitler soon realized that he couldn't win the war. On May 7, 1945, Germany surrendered. The war in Europe was over! That was what we wanted to hear!

Why Your Grandma Talks Funny

Hooray! Very soon we saw the jeeps and trucks—that was something! In Germany, we never saw a car, of course.

The American soldiers were so kind to us! We didn't know what to expect because they weren't German, but they treated us like their own. They gave us candy and chocolate! They also had this long package, and it wasn't candy or chocolate. We didn't know what it was. We opened it and saw a thin, bendable piece of something about the length of our fingers.

"Try it! You put it in your mouth and start chewing it, but don't swallow it," said one soldier.

More Chewing Gum, Please!

"Mmmm," said Art.

"Wow! You can chew it, and it never goes away!" I exclaimed!

"Does it last forever?" asked Tillie.

"Ha, Ha, Ha," the soldiers chuckled, "no, but it sure is fun, isn't it?"

We had never had gum before. That was so special for us! So, the next time the soldiers came, we just wanted that chewing gum!

It was now July, and we were staying north of Berlin in a town called Schwerin and even though the war was over, the Russians now owned the piece of land where we were staying. The Americans told us, "Don't be afraid. They may be mean, but they cannot do bad things to you like they did during the war." We worked in the fields and raised sugar beets. There was a big Russian soldier on a horse, and he would ride up and down the fields. You didn't dare stretch or talk to your neighbor because he would get his whip out; however, they did give us flour, bread and meat each week. We could get milk every day when we milked the cows.

One day, we were getting low on grain to make bread and meals. Right across the street was a beautiful, fancy house—filled with grain! The Russian soldiers would stand guard outside of the house to make sure no one helped themselves to all the grain stored inside these nice homes. Artur, trying not to show his dislike for the Russian soldiers, walked over to the guard and did some bartering for some grain. I don't know what he said or how he did it, but he walked away with a pail full of grain and a big smile on his face!

Sometimes, the Russians would make it so hard on us, and we were fearful they would take our cows so my brother Art and some of his friends dug a huge pit in the ground. They hid our milking cow in this huge pit and piled the hay up around the cow so the Russians wouldn't see it. I don't know how the cow stayed so still and quiet, but it must've worked because they never took our cow!

CHAPTER
10

Hope at Last

*Schwerin, Germany
to Backnang, Germany
July 1947*

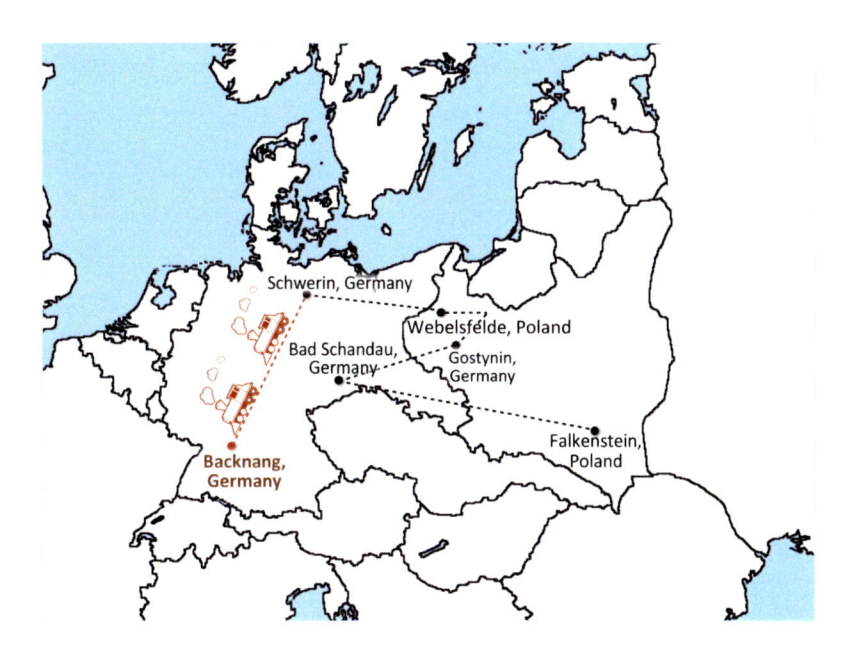

After two years of living in Schwerin under Soviet control, we knew we did not want to stay here for the rest of our lives. We for sure wanted to immigrate to another country. We were able to contact Mother's sister and her family, Philip and Mathilde Rauch, who had been able to get to the British zone of Germany. My cousin Isle reached out to the Mennonite Central Committee for us in hopes of starting a new life. The MCC worked with Mennonites in different countries to help bring other Mennonites and refugees to a safe place.

One day we received a letter from the Mennonite Central Committee.

"What does it say? Open it!" Tille exclaimed.

Waiting in anticipation, we all huddled around Mother as she held the envelope in her hands. She just looked at it. I felt her hesitation. *What would the letter say?* This letter could possibly be the answer we were longing for. We watched as Mother slipped her finger under the flap and broke the seal. She pulled out the letter and read it. Indeed, it was the answer we were hoping for! *Wunderbar!* We had been approved, and they were going to help us.

They gave us a couple of different options for immigrating. We could choose America, Canada, Argentina or Paraguay; all we had to do was write back. This was another big decision that Mother had to make without the help of Father. Should we leave Germany and all of our family, the life and home we love or should we pursue immigration and a fresh start in a new place, new language, new friends and no family?

"I am going to write back and ask to go to Canada. Your Aunt Elizabeth is already there, and that would be so great to be with family. They could help us learn the language, show us all around and help us get settled," said Mother.

We soon learned that Canada was not accepting any

refugees or displaced persons at that time because they had already reached their limit on how many refugees they could take. Mother didn't seem much interested after that news. With Canada no longer an option for us, any country we chose would be just as good as the next one.

We had heard that Paraguay was known as the "Green Hell." Their dense rain forest and primitive living with no roads was not very appealing to Mother. Since Argentina was so far from Canada and our family, America seemed like a good option. We chose to just take it one step at a time and decide on our final destination further down the "road" of immigration.

Our first step of immigration was getting across the Russian line and into Western Germany. This was quite the experience! We had to take a train to get to Germany.

Passenger trains were sparse, and trains going west were even more sparse. The Russian army used a lot of passenger trains to help in their military so that made catching a train very difficult.

"Stay close," said Mother. "Artur, keep the bags close."

The crowd was so big that everyone was shoulder to shoulder. As we tried to make our way to the train, we kept bumping into people.

"*Entschuldigen Sie,* excuse me, *Entschuldigen Sie,*" was all we really heard from the hundreds of people rushing through the train depot.

I guess we weren't the only ones who didn't want to stay here, I thought to myself. *Hope we can all get on the same train together. These trains are just packed! People everywhere, and, oh my, that family only has one small satchel. They must've lost everything like us.*

I didn't really see a lot of men, fathers, that is. The mothers were taking the responsibility again, and I recognized the same facial expressions that I saw during our travels in the wagon train. The loud train whistle blew.

"Hurry," cried Mother. "Stay together!"

We all hopped on the train, and it was so crowded! Mothers, boys and even small children were hanging on for dear life halfway out of the train. Everybody wanted to escape the Russian oppression.

Hope at Last

But, with God's grace and provision, we made it. We crossed over into German territory. At first, they let us off in Backnang, a southwest German city, at a Mennonite immigration camp. We lived in a leather factory. There were four families in a room, but we had bunk beds which we were really thankful for. We had to stay there until our immigration papers were ready to go over to America. Mother helped with the cooking and cleaning, Art worked in the leather factory, I worked with the spinning wheel and Tillie attended school. At night, I would crawl into the bunk bed. Art and I stayed up later than Tillie and Mother most nights and talked about so many different things. This night it was a more serious tone, I could tell Art was getting concerned.

"My arms hurt so bad," said Art. "Those animal skins are so hard to pull and stretch."

"I bet," I agreed. "The spinning wheel isn't too tough, but you do have to pay attention."

"Remember when we slept for weeks all curled up in our bumpy wagon?" Art asked.

"*Ja*, this bed is so nice. But sometimes I wish we could be in OUR beds in OUR home. I miss our home." I was trying to hold back tears and sound brave, but I was feeling a little homesick.

"What happens if we don't get approved for immigration?" asked Art.

I shook my head back and forth. "I'm not sure," I said.

"I hope we don't have to be here long."

"Me too," I agreed.

At the camp in Backnang, there was a German preacher. He would have Bible studies with us teenagers. One night we were gathered together, ready to hear the preaching. We listened to him as he taught God's Word. He really stressed that salvation was through Jesus' dying on the cross to save us from our sins so we could go to Heaven one day. I remember the preacher talked about the 23rd Psalm—the Lord is my Shepherd. He told us we needed to take the Lord as our Shepherd and our Savior. I knew I needed Him. I needed a Helper with all the things we had been through. I needed Somebody. So that's when I acknowledged I was a sinner, repented from my sin and thanked Jesus for dying on the cross to pay for my sins. I asked Him to come into my heart and take me to Heaven when I die. That's when I trusted the Lord as my Savior, and now the Lord is MY Shepherd!

CHAPTER
11

The Long Voyage

*Backnang, Germany
to Rotterdam, Netherlands
November 1949*

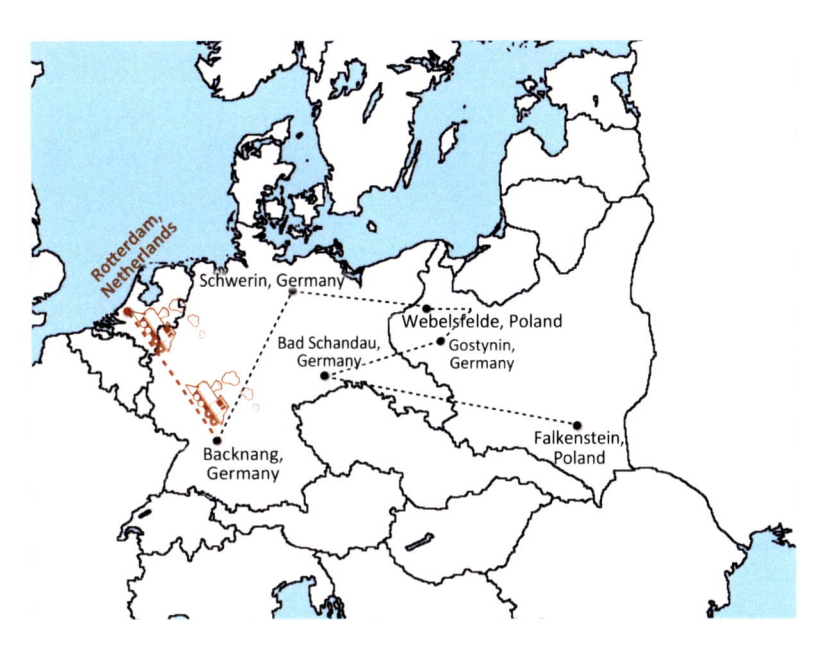

"Christine Bachmann?"

"Ja?"

"You're wanted in the administration office. Right this way, please."

Mother followed the clerk into the office. We weren't

sure what was going on in there. Finally, Mother walked out. She never really showed much expression on her face, so we didn't know if it was good news or bad news.

"*Kinder,* we have been approved. We must get our things together. In two days' time we will be taking a train to the Netherlands. There we will choose a boat that will take us to a new country. I must pray for the next several days for us to choose the right boat."

"How can we afford tickets?" I asked.

"There are Mennonite churches everywhere. Some very kind people in those churches donated money to help Mennonites in Europe immigrate to freedom. We will work for them until our debts are paid in full."

"*Mutter,* will *Vater* get to come too?" Tillie asked.

"He is being so brave. He is going to stay in Poland and protect all the Germans," said *Mutter.*

In just two short days, it was moving day again. We took a train from Backnang, Germany, to the Netherlands.

On November 25, 1949, we lined up in Rotterdam, Netherlands, and like so many others there in that port, looked out at all of the boats. Some were pulling into the dock and others were leaving.

"To Paraguay, to Argentina, to America, to China… look at all these boats!" exclaimed Art.

It was hard not to question Mother, but we all wanted to know which boat she thought the Lord would want us to get on. We hardly knew anything about these countries.

"I hope *Mutter* picks America," said Tillie.

The Long Voyage

"Why, Tillie?" I asked.

"Because we can get lots of chewing gum there!"

"*Ja*, and those soldiers were so nice," added Art.

I could see hesitancy on some people's faces. No one was quite sure about boarding a boat that would cross the ocean. However, it was our only means of transportation.

Carrying all that we owned, we loaded on to the *SS Leerdam*. This boat was sailing to America. It was a freight boat, so it took much longer to get there. We were on the boat for the next fourteen days.

"Here, Tillie, stay close," I said. "It's cold in here!"

"My tummy feels weird, Nelly."

"I know, mine too." *And so must everyone else's too,* I thought to myself. People would get seasick, and right there over the edge of the boat…eww, you know what would happen next!

After about two weeks of sailing, I woke up one morning to the sound of excited chatter.

"What is it, *Mutter*?" I asked.

I got up from where I was sleeping, and the cold December air bit me in the face. *Brrrrr. It sure is cold,* I thought. *"Wonder what the big green statue is over in the harbor?"* I mused.

"Ladies and gentlemen, as we arrive in New York, you will find to your left a tall green statue. May I introduce you to Lady Liberty, America's symbol of freedom. She was a gift from France in 1878. From the ground to the top of her torch, the statue measures 93 meters and weighs 204 metric

Why Your Grandma Talks Funny

tons. Inscribed on the base of the statue you will find these words:

Give me your tired, your poor, your huddled masses yearning to breathe free. The wretched refuse of your teeming shore. Send these, the homeless, tempest-tossed to me, I lift my lamp beside the golden door!"

We were extremely glad to see the Statue of Liberty because maybe now we would have a home again. It had been ten years—1939 to 1949—that we went from one place to the next place. During that time, we went to school for maybe four years. There was no home for us. We were very thankful to be in America. Mother was telling us all about America from what she had heard from her sister in Canada and was very adamant that we learn the language and work hard so that we could contribute to our new country.

I remembered the quote the speaker told us that was inscribed on the base of the statue. It described the people who were on the boat, including us, as *tired, poor, yearning to breathe free, homeless, tempest-tossed.* Although we breathed a small sigh of relief, we were still unsure of what awaited us in this new country.

CHAPTER
12

A New Adventure

Ellis Island
December 1949

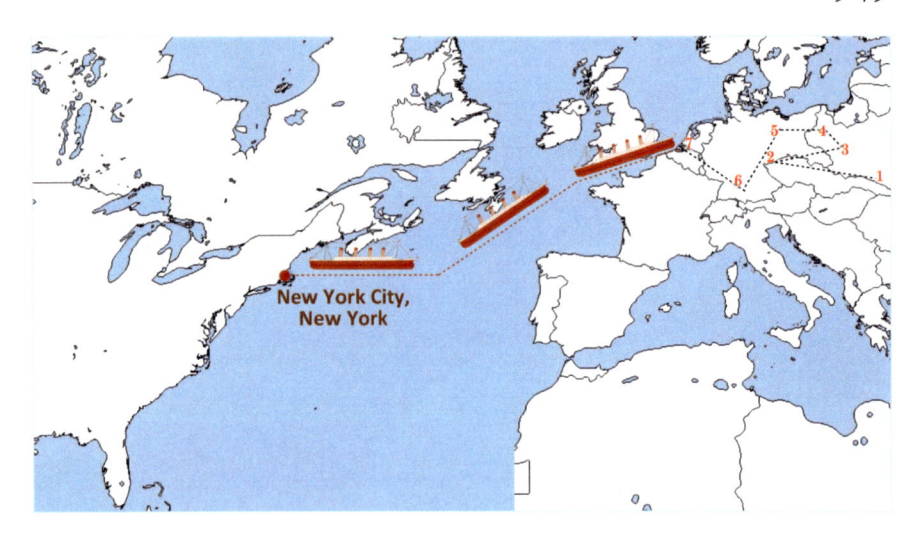

"Ladies and gentlemen, as you exit the *SS Leerdam*, please gather all of your belongings, and watch your step as you enter the dock. For immigration, you will go to the tall brick building to your left."

We had to go there to get all of our paperwork approved to enter America. As soon as we entered the building, we saw the American flag. Some people stood, looked at it and removed their hats in respect. We started up the large staircase towards the main floor. The building was very crowded.

A New Adventure

There were people everywhere—not just people from our boat, but from several other boats as well. I started to feel overwhelmed as I began to listen to all of the people around me. I couldn't understand them all. There were many different languages being spoken at the same time.

"You will need to fill out this form. Each child has his own form as well. I will ask you a list of questions, please answer as best as possible."

"Religion?"

"Mennonite."

"Baptism?"

"*Ja.*"

"Any health-related issues such as impetigo, diabetes, heart disease?"

"*Nein.*"

"Please proceed to this line here. The immigration office will take your papers from you there."

The lines were so long. We got in line and we waited and waited. As we waited, I looked around, taking in all of the scenes. I saw families getting medical examinations. Doctors were checking them for health problems and diseases. I watched as a child or mother failed the examination and was ripped away from his family and forced into quarantine. I saw tired people. I saw sad people. I saw happy people. Everyone here was from a different background, different situation, but we all had one goal—freedom. Finally, our turn to talk to the immigration officer came. We gave him the forms we had filled out. He looked them over and approved them!

Why Your Grandma Talks Funny

"This way, *kinder*," said Mother.

I don't know how she knew what to do next or where to go, but we just tried to be helpful and patient.

"We need to find Train B23 for Pennsylvania. Let's walk this way. Stay together."

"All aboard!"

Here we were boarding yet another train. These trains were much nicer than any other train we had been on in the last ten years. We arrived in Pennsylvania and stayed there for a couple of weeks, and then we were on our way to Iowa.

We felt the train slow down and eventually stop. We stepped outside and quickly saw that we were in the middle of no-

A New Adventure

where! There were crop fields all around us. We waited for our sponsor, but no one came.

"They have dropped us off here in the middle of nowhere to die!" Mother exclaimed with a sigh.

Remember, we had just come through war. We still didn't know who we could trust and who we couldn't trust.

"Excuse me, Christine Bachmann?"

"*Ja.*"

"Hello, my name is Lester Miller. I am here to help you."

A small sense of relief came over Mother's expression, but I could tell she was still a little upset from thinking we were brought here to die.

"I have a horse and buggy right over here. Are these your things?"

"*Ja, danke.*"

"We get to ride in this?" Tillie exclaimed. The buggy was so much nicer than our old rickety wagon back in Germany.

"Can I ride in front with you, Mr. Miller?" asked Art.

"Of course you can! I've arranged some homes for each of you to help out in. I can drop you off as we drive if that's okay. The farms aren't too far from one another, and the nice thing is, all of us farmers attend the same church on Sunday so you'll get to see each other then," he concluded. For the next year, these farms became our homes as we paid our debts to Mr. Miller.

Mother worked at the Maplecrest Turkey Factory in Wellman, Iowa, just west of Kalona, and lived with an Amish family. Working at the turkey factory was hard and nasty work, but Mother never complained. I worked for an Amish family around their farm. Artur was a farmhand for Mr. Miller and Tillie was at a different household. It was not fun for all of us to be split up while living and working at different households, but we did get to see each other at church on Sunday. We all attended East Union Mennonite Church. We loved Sundays because we were able to see our family and learn the English language. It was not easy to sit still and listen to a sermon in English when all we understood was German, but Mother encouraged us that we were living in America and were now Americans. We must learn the English language, work and contribute and pledge our allegiance to the American flag.

By late 1950, Christine, my mother, purchased a house in Kalona. There she made a new home. I went to college in Iowa City to learn how to become an x-ray technician, Artur stayed on as a farmhand in Kalona and learned carpentry while also working in a cheese factory at Gingrich Farms. Tillie finished school and stayed close to Mother.

In 1950, I found a husband—or maybe he found me! Because of my mother's trust in the Lord, He directed our path, and we were so very thankful for Him leading us over here! I am thankful that through the darkest and scariest of paths fleeing Russian oppression, the Lord was our Shepherd, and my mother trusted in Him!

EPILOGUE

Why Grandma's Story Is Special to Us

Grandma's story is incredible. But it is what happened from here that has made her the amazing woman that we remember today. In the next part of her story, she took all of the lessons from her difficult and humble beginnings and went on to live a full and fulfilling life as an American citizen, wife, mother, grandmother and great-grandmother.

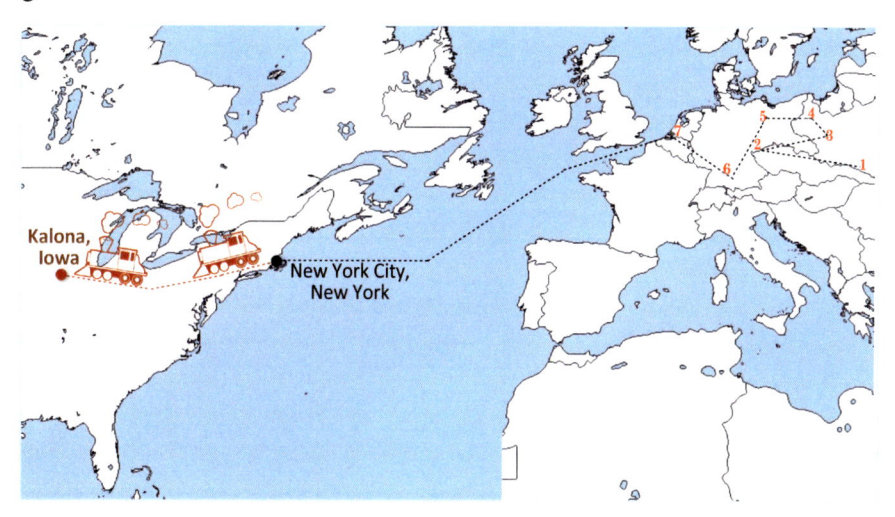

Within one year of arriving in Kalona, Iowa, the Bachmann family was able to work off their passage to America. Great-Grandma Bachmann purchased a small house in

Kalona, and the family made it their new home. They never heard from their father again. He was declared dead somewhere in Europe. Grandma often spoke of their desire to become good citizens and truly contribute to their new country by learning the language and working hard.

As time went by, Grandma met a fellow Mennonite young man named John Christner. John was the son of Kalona farmers. They married on June 28, 1953. God blessed them with a son, Steve, in 1956; a daughter, Joyce, in 1957; and another daughter, Heidi, in 1964. In 1965, Grandpa bought a small farm on the outskirts of Kalona, which is where they resided until 2003. Grandma had never driven a vehicle before; but, on the farm, she needed to learn to drive. As the story goes, Grandma's first lessons were quite unsuccessful as Grandpa tried teaching her to drive with a manual transmission! Grandpa had to buy an automatic vehicle just so Grandma could drive it!

Along with the move, there were also spiritual changes taking place in the Christner family. Both Grandpa and Grandma had been saved as young people. After marriage, they continued to attend the Mennonite church in Kalona along with the Bachmann and Christner families. But one day, Grandpa and Grandma were invited to attend a Bible study in Wayland, Iowa. This Bible study, along with his own personal Bible reading, opened Grandpa's eyes to many truths which he had not been aware of before. He was beginning to realize that the teachings of the Mennonite church were not enough for him to grow into the Christian he had

Why Grandma's Story Is Special to Us

been learning about through the Bible. This began a quest for a church that would truly line up with the Bible truths that began to burn within his heart. Grandpa and Grandma joined a Bible church in Wayland, Iowa. But once again, he still felt something was missing! He had been reading and learning that Christians have a responsibility to reach other people for Christ.

During this time, Grandpa was reading the Bible and being influenced by Independent Baptist preaching and *The Sword of the Lord* newspaper. He and four other men, along with their families, decided to leave the Bible church and begin their own independent, fundamental, Bible-believing Baptist church. They found an old Presbyterian church for sale on Marion Avenue in Washington, Iowa, and Grandpa himself financed the purchasing of this building. It was in 1973 that Marion Avenue Baptist Church was founded!

They immediately began searching for a pastor. Different preachers would fill the pulpit on Sundays to preach God's Word to these hungry people. In the meantime, they were busy trying to reach others with the gospel of Jesus Christ and bring them to church. One of the visiting preachers suggested the church call on a young preacher from North Carolina by the name of Larry Brown. Within the very same year that the church began, he became the pastor of this growing group of people.

Grandpa and Grandma were not only founding members of Marion Avenue Baptist Church, but they were *involved* members. They sang in the choir, taught Sunday school, went soul winning, started a bus route, handled the church finances and opened their home to visiting preachers, evangelists, missionaries and college tour groups that came through the church doors. They served in many of these ministries up until they were in their seventies. Their faithfulness to each other, the Lord, their church and their pastor continues to be a wonderful example to the generations of their family. At this time, their children, grandchildren and great-grandchildren are still experiencing the blessings of the spiritual choices Grandpa and Grandma made many years ago.

We are thankful the Lord protected and spared Grandma's life as she fled Europe with her family from the horrors of war and evils of communism. We are thankful God blessed her bountifully in her new home in America. We are also grateful that Grandma did not let the hardships of her early life produce a "victim" mentality in her adult years. In fact, Grandma was the exact opposite of a victim. She was an overcomer and demonstrated her gratefulness for her American freedom by serving the Lord, her family and others until God took her home in September of 2007. She was beloved by her family, her church family, members of the community, and frankly, by all who came to know her.

She and Grandpa built a life—a heritage—which would live on, not only to demonstrate the beauty of the American dream, but also to further the kingdom of God. We see the hand of God throughout her entire story, and it should teach us patience and courage. It also serves as a wonderful

Why Grandma's Story Is Special to Us

reminder of the ripple affect just one life can have on future generations. Let us trust the Lord with our lives and rest in the knowledge that He will safely navigate us through each situation or circumstance that comes our way just as He did for Grandma.

John and Nelly Christner on their wedding day

Christine, Nelly, Artur and Mathilde Bachmann

Inset: Nelly

Above: Christine Bachmann
Inset: Christine with suggested sponsor, Lester Miller

Above: Christine at the Maplecrest Turkey Factory

Below: John and Nelly's farmouse, Kalona, Iowa

John and Nelly with Steve, Joyce and Heidi Christner

My Mother's Trunk
by Mrs. Joyce Anglea

My mother was a German teenager during Hitler's conquest for Europe. I grew up hearing her stories of air raids, blackouts and her family's journey to America.

Several years ago she gave me an old wooden trunk that had come over on the boat with her from Germany. I decided to put in this trunk heirlooms that I would someday give to my children. Then I thought of several things my mother taught me that I also wanted to hand down to them. So I gathered six items to put in my trunk that would remind me of those things. These are the items and what they represent to me.

A 1957 Chevrolet ~
You Can Trust Your Daddy

One summer evening, our family went to visit some friends who lived in the country. Although it was sunny when we went, it was foggy on the way home. I was very frightened and told my mom that I was scared. She very calmly said, "Daddy is a good driver, and he will get us home safely."

At that moment, my dad became my hero. My mom trusted him, and I could too. This made a huge impression on me. When I came to the inevitable crossroads that all teenagers come to in their life, I chose to go God's way because it was Dad's way. I shudder to think what my life would be like had my mom not instilled in me this trust for my dad.

A Weekly Calendar ~
Make Your Husband's Life Your Life

I love being in the ministry. However, I experienced some very difficult times during our early years.

During those times, I would go to my mom with my frustrations. She never felt sorry for me. I could not figure out why; she was my mother, after all. Then I remembered the calendar she kept in her laundry room. As a farm wife, she had to help my dad with the livestock. On the pages of this calendar, she recorded important information, like when a new litter of piglets was born or when she gave them their vaccinations. Farm chores are not glamorous, yet she never complained about them. Her husband was a farmer, and she made farm life her life. I determined I should be happy to do the same for my preacher husband!

My Second Grade Class Picture ~
You Cannot Run Away from Your Problems

The most horrible event happened to me while in the second grade. One day a girl in my class announced that the next day was going to be "Be Mean to Joyce Christner Day." I was horrified! Whatever was I going to do? I immediately went home and told my mom. She very simply said, "That's okay. If they don't want to play with you, you just go find someone else to play with." I was not all that excited about her solution to solve my problem, but today I understand the wisdom behind it. By telling me to go and play with someone else, she was telling me that there will always be problems in life. You have to face them and figure out a way to solve them.

My Mom and Dad's Wedding Picture ~
It Is Better to Get Along Than to Get Your Way

My mother loved my dad's family. I remember her laughing and having a good time with them at family gatherings. I remember how my dad would say that he never heard my mom say one bad thing about his mother. This never really hit home with me until I was married. While my roots were in the Midwest, my husband's roots ran very deep in the South. There were so many differences in our families, I couldn't believe it. There were times when these differences could have been (and even sometimes were) a source of conflict. It was the fact that my mom got along with her in-laws that I determined I needed to get along with mine.

Kopftuch ~
The Cure for What Ails You

Whenever my mother was working, she wore a bandana tied around her head. She called it by its German name—*kopftuch*. Whenever we kids were moping around, her cure was "Get up and do something, and then you will feel better." It always worked!

My Mother's Trunk

When I was first married, I had a lot of ills. There were times I wanted to walk around and have a pity party. Then I would remember my mom in her *kopftuch* and would get busy. Then I would feel better. Many years ago we had a woman in our church who was suffering from a disorder with a big long name that simply meant "I don't feel good." I thought to myself, "If you had a mom like mine, you wouldn't have this problem!"

When I think of the difficulties my mom faced before coming to America and the difficulties she faced after she arrived, I marvel. And the most amazing thing is that she did it without getting a wounded spirit. Proverbs 18:14 says, *"The spirit of a man will sustain his infirmity; but a wounded spirit who can bear?"*

We all have our share of infirmities. We all have our chances to become bitter. Mom didn't and I don't want to either. So, for the finishing touch, I put a pretty, crocheted doily on top. It is a reminder that no matter how difficult life may be, we cannot allow ourselves to get a wounded, bitter spirit.

Recently we discovered the name of the ship that my mother and her family came over on. We were also able to get a copy of the manifest of in-bound passengers. Beside my grandmother's name was a list of her family's baggage which included "3 Tr." One of those trunks is now sitting in my bedroom. I want it to be more than an antique heirloom. I want it to be a legacy that is passed down from generation to generation!

About the Authors

Hannah lives in an all-boy home with her husband, Jason Walker, and four boys ranging from four to fourteen years of age. They live in Elgin, Illinois, and attend Northwest Bible Baptist Church where Jason has been the principal of Northwest Baptist Academy since 2004. Hannah enjoys serving in several ministries of NBBC as well as helping her husband in the academy when needed. She enjoys riding bikes with her boys, walks with her husband and puzzles.

About the Authors

Abbie is married to Alan Miller and enjoys looking after her two girls ages seven and four. Alan is an assistant pastor at Faith Baptist Church in Bourbonnais, Illinois. Abbie works alongside her husband in Children's Church as well as other ministries of FBC. She enjoys family bike rides in the summer, shopping and decorating.

Leah is a busy mom to three little boys ages four, three and one. She is married to assistant pastor Pete Cavanaugh, and they make their home in the southern state of Mississippi. They enjoy serving on staff at Bethel Baptist Church. Leah serves in various ministries of BBC and is the nursery director. She enjoys being outside with her boys and gardening.

Cherith and her husband, Isaiah Hanson, are currently on deputation. They are answering God's call to be missionaries to the needy people of Panama. Cherith enjoys creating projects on her Cricut, baking, cake decorating and long walks with her husband.

Is the Lord Your Shepherd?

The greatest story ever told is about Jesus Christ. Jesus' story is a very important one for you.

God's Word teaches us that all people are sinners.

Romans 3:23, *"For all have sinned...."* Sin is in your nature. You do not have to teach little ducks to swim; they know how because it is their nature. You did not have to be taught how to lie, be selfish or disobey your parents; that is your nature.

God's Word also teaches us that we have to pay for our sin.

Romans 6:23, *"For the wages of sin is death...."* That is very sad and frightening. Someday you will die, but your life will not end. You will go to one of two places to live for all eternity. One of the places is called Hell and is a place of eternal dying; it is a place of fire; it is a place of suffering. That is what you owe for your sin. You have sinned against God, and the payment for that sin is separation from God forever in that awful place.

God's Word has good news for you.

It is the greatest story ever told. Romans 5:8 *"...Christ died for us."* The good news is the Gospel of Jesus Christ. Jesus left Heaven and came to earth and died, was buried and rose again to pay for your sin. Yes, Jesus paid the price that you owe for your sin! You may wonder why He did that. He did that because He and His Father, God, love you very much. John 3:16, *"For God so loved the world, that He gave His only begotten Son..."*

God's Word makes it clear that you can know for sure that you will go to Heaven when you die.

Romans 6:23, *"...the gift of God is eternal life through Jesus Christ our Lord."* Heaven is the place of eternal life. Heaven is where God and Jesus both live. It is a wonderful place. It is the place that you can go because Jesus died for you.

God's Word is very specific about who gets to go to Heaven.

Jesus told Nicodemus that in order to see or enter Heaven he had to be born again, so do you. Being born again is the result of trusting Jesus for salvation. Romans 10:13, *"For whosoever shall call upon the name of the Lord shall be saved."* You must ask Jesus to save you. You must be serious and confess to Him that you are a sinner and that you believe He died to take you to Heaven.

God's Word tells us we can pray, and God will hear us.

Are you a sinner? Do you want to be saved from eternal death in Hell? Pray to God; pray something like this from your heart: "Dear God, I admit I am a sinner, and I deserve to go to Hell, but I believe Jesus died for me. I believe Jesus paid for my sin. Jesus, I receive You now as my Saviour. Please come into my heart and save me. Thank You for dying for me."

If you prayed that prayer and meant it, please let us know by calling 815.933.9400 and tell us you received Jesus as your Saviour. That is the greatest news we could possibly hear.

Refugee Files and Translations

IX-19-16 - 4   1/13
- Refugee Files
Bachmann, A. - H.

CASE CLOSED - Migrated to U.S. Nov. 24, 1949
1949   U. S. Case # __117__

CROSS REFERENCE SHEET

Name or Subject   Birthdate   Address

BACHMANN, Christine Schweitzer   April 17, 1901   U. S. Zone, Germany
   "   Nelly   May 14, 1929
   "   Artur   July 27, 1930
   "   Mathilde   August 29, 1935
   "   Marie   February 3, 1889

                                        Birth Place: Falkenstein, Poland

Regarding   Sponsor

U. S. immigration   Lester B. Miller
                                         Route 1
                                         Kalona, Iowa
V. D. Quota

Affidavit of Support forwarded to M. Brunk Jan. 10, 1949

SEE

Name or Subject Filed Under

Personal Data sheet # 117   A. J. Beachy (2-1-50)
                                    Ernest Lehman (6-12-50)
Lester B. Miller (1949)(1950)

Marie Brunk (1-10-49)(8-8-49)(8-18-49)(8-31)(9-10-49) (9-23-49) (11-4-49)

Paul L. Ruth to Marie Brunk (9-6-49) to Menno Travel (11-2-49)

Paul Ruth (9-30-49) (10-4-49)(11/26/49)   Mrs. Christine Bachmann (1950)(1948)

Menn. Bib. Seminary (12-2-49)

Expense Statement from Menno T.S. Amsterdam (11-26-49)
                                                          Doreen Harms (5.16.52)
Menno Travel, Amsterdam to A.Voth (11-28-49)(11/27/49)

To Whom It May Concern (12-10-49)
Elma Esau (12-13-49)
Business Office (12-12-49) (1-17-50)
  Cable from Marie Brunk (9-18-49)

File cross reference form under name or subject at top of the sheet. Describe
matter for identification purposes. The papers themselves should be filed
under name or subject after "SEE".

81

Why Your Grandma Talks Funny

Going to U.S.A through Stuttgart Consulate on 25 Nov. 49.

Bachmann Christine

Name des Familienhauptes

MCC/249

ALLGEMEINER M.C.C. FRAGEBOGEN

A. PERSONALIEN

Name: *Bachmann Christine*   Mädchenname: *Schweitzer*

Geburtsdatum: *17.4.01*   Geburtsort: (Dorf/Stadt) *Falkenstein* (Land *Galizien*)

Verhältnis zum Familienhaupt: (z.B. Sohn, Tochter, Frau, usw.) _____

Kinder unter 18 Jahre: (Nur auf Fragebogen des "Familienhauptes" eingutragen)

Name	Geburtsdaten	Geburtsort
1. Bachmann Mathilde	29.1.1930	Falkenstein
2. Arthur		
3. Nelly		
4.		
5.		
6.		

B. RELIGION & GEMEINDE

1. Welcher Konfession gehören Sie an: (evg.) menot.
2. Sind Sie getauft: *Ja*   Kinder oder Erwachsenentaufe *Kindertaufe*
   Wann: *21.4.*   Wo: *Falkenstein*   Von wem *J. Gorgon Pfarrer*
   Warum: *Weil es die Konfession so verlangte und auch den Glauben*
3. Welcher Gemeinde gehören Sie an: (Kirchengemeinde/Brüdergemeinde, usw.) *Kirchengemeinde*
4. Falls Aufnahme in die Gemeinde nicht durch Taufe erfolgte, beschreiben Sie diese näher: (z.B. Durch Heirat, Handschlag, Brief, usw.) *Heirat*
5. Wann wurden Sie aufgenommen: *1928*   Wo: *Lemberg*   Von wem *Gemeinde Lemberg*
6. Waren Ihre beiden Eltern Mennoniten: *nein*
7. Sind Sie in der Lage sonntäglich mennonitischen Andachten beizuwohnen: *ja*
   Wenn nicht, welche Möglichkeit bietet sich Ihnen: _____
   Nehmen Sie an nicht-mennonitischem Gottesdienst teil: *ja*   An Welchem *Methodisten*
   Wann besuchten Sie zum letzten Mal regelmässig mennonitischen Gottesdienst:
   1939   Wo: *Lemberg – Falkenstein*
8. Sind Sie Mitglied oder Anhänger irgend einer andern Glaubensgemeinschaft: (z.B. Jehovas Zeugen, Adventisten, usw.) *nein*   Welche: _____

Refugee Files and Translations

- 2 -

C. BERUFLICHES & GESUNDHEITLICHES

1. Wie viel Jahre Schulbildung haben Sie gehabt: _8_ Wo:(Land) _Galizien_
2. Erlernter Beruf: _Hausfrau_ Nebenberuf: _Landwirtin_
3. Hauptbeschäftigung vor 1940: _Hausf._ Heutige Beschäftigung: _keine_
4. Wieviel verdienen Sie monatlich: _nichts_
5. Wovon lebten Sie nach dem Zusammenbruch und vor der Währungsreform: _Ich besaß etwas Geld und auch von eigenem Verdienst u. Lagerverpflg_
6. Sind Sie nach heutigen Verhältnissen mit Ihrer Wohnung zufrieden: _ja_
7. Sind Sie körperlich gesund: _ja_ Wenn nicht, beschreiben Sie Ihr Leiden oder Gebrechen: _____
8. Sind Ihre Kinder unter 18 Jahre gesund:(nur für das Familienhaupt) _ja_
   Wenn nicht, beschreiben Sie Leiden: _____

D. AUSWANDERUNG

1. Möchten Sie um jeden Preis auswandern: _ja_ Welches ist der Hauptgrund: _Es geht um die Existenzmöglichkeit_
   Andere Gründe: _____
2. In welches Land:(erste Wahl) _U.S.A._ (2te Wahl) _Canada_ _Deutschland_
3. Wenn nach Canada:
   a) Haben Sie einen Bürgen: _nein_ Wie sind Sie mit ihm verwandt: _____
   b) Name und Adresse des Bürgen: _____
   c) Ihre Herausrufungsnummer ist: _____
   d) Sind Sie vor der I.R.O. Kommission gewesen: _ja_ Wann: _Okt 48_ Wo: _Backnang_
      Was war das Ergebnis: (Angenommen/Abgelehnt) _Unentschieden_
   e) Falls schon vor canadischer Dienststelle erschienen, weshalb wurden Sie
      Abgesagt: _____ Wann: _____
      Zurückgestellt: _____ Wann: _____ Auf wie lange: _____
4. Wenn nach Süd-Amerika, in welches Land:(Paraguay/Uruguay) _____
   Wenn Grund Verwandtschaft ist, bitte Verwandtschaftsgrad angeben: _____
   Sonstige besondere Gründe:(Sprungbrett nach Canada,usw.) _____
5. Wenn nach U.S.A., aus welchen Gründen: _Der Existenz wegen, Glaubensfreiheit und Kriegswegen_

Why Your Grandma Talks Funny

> Benutzen Sie diese Seite für weitere Angaben und Ausführungen:
>
> Nach U.S.A. sollten wir eine Bürgschaft haben u. zwar von Sester B. Miller Kalona Jowa St. l. U.S.A.
>
> Wir haben uns 48 auf die Volksdeutsche Quotte in Stuttgart gemeldet und die N° 139 erhalten.
>
> Und meine Schwägerin Marie Bachmann hat die N° 138.

(See translation of pages 82-85 on pages 93-96.)

Refugee Files and Translations

17. Nennen Sie Verwandte, wenn auch noch so weitläufig, unter den Flüchtlingen in Deutschland (SEHR WICHTIG):

a) Name: *Lang*   Vorname: *Amalie*   Geburtsdatum: *7.10.1896*   Verwandtschaftsgrad: *Schwägerin*
Anschrift in Deutschland: *Aub im Grabfeld 58 (13)a Kr. Königshofen, Bayern*

b) Name: _____ Vorname: _____ Geburtsdatum: _____ Verwandtschaftsgrad: _____
Anschrift in Deutschland: _____

c) Name: _____ Vorname: _____ Geburtsdatum: _____ Verwandtschaftsgrad: _____
Anschrift in Deutschland: _____

d) Name: _____ Vorname: _____ Geburtsdatum: _____ Verwandtschaftsgrad: _____
Anschrift in Deutschland: _____

Vollständige Adresse:
Christine Bachmann
in Backnang
Lager Leba
b. Stuttgart

Datum: *10.4.1940*
Unterschrift: *Christine Bachmann*

NUR FUER MCC

a) Reference Letter:
b) Personal Interview: *Has spouse in U.S. Husband was men. Children men.*

Ausgewandert im Dezember 49 nach USA

Signature MCC Representative: _____   Place of Interview: *Bkg*   Date: *9.4.49*

Why Your Grandma Talks Funny

```
HAVE DECIDED TO GO TO PARAGUAY                    Case No.  US 33

                    PERSONAL DATA SHEET           1948

NAME                        BIRTHPLACE                    BIRTHDATE

Bachmann, Christina Schweizer   Falkenstein, Poland   Apr. 4, 1901
Bachmann, Nelly                       "              May 14, 1929
Bachmann, Artur                       "              July 27, 1930
Bachmann, Matilda                     "              Aug. 29, 1935
Bachmann, Marie (sister-in-law)       "              Feb. 2, 1889

FAMILY BACKGROUND

        They are Galician Mennonites. Mrs. Bachmann was born Evangelical
        but has been assimilated by the Mennonites.

HEALTH CONDITIONS

        They are all physically and mentally sound.

OCCUPATION

        They are an agricultural family and are all well acquainted
        with land work. Artur is now working in a leather factory
        and Nelly works in a meat market and hotel. Marie Bachmann
        does housework and land work.

RELATIVES

        They have relatives in Minn. but are not in contact with them.

COUNTRY PREFERRED

        United States or Canada

ELIGIBILITY FOR U.S. IMMIGRATION

        They have been living in the US Zone only since June 1947.
        They have a Polish birth certificate for the father, Rudolf
        Bachmann, who has been missing since Jan. 1945. Mrs. Bach-
        mann has her original birth certificate, as does Marie Bach-
        mann, the sister-in-law.

REMARKS
```

Refugee Files and Translations

```
                                                      U.S. Case No. 117
NAME                     BIRTHPLACE                   BIRTHDATE

Bachmann, Christine (Schweitzer)  Falkenstein, Poland  Apr. 17, 1901
    "     Nelly                        "               May 14, 1929
    "     Artur                        "               July 27, 1930
    "     Mathilde                     "               Aug. 29, 1935
    "     Marie (sister-in-law)        "               Feb. 3, 1889
```

FAMILY BACKGROUND
    All are Mennonites except Mrs. Christine Bachmann who is Protestnat. They speak German and Polish.

HEALTH CONDITION
    All are of good mental and physical health

OCCUPATION
    Mrs. Bachmann is not only a housekeeper but has had 30 years of experience in farmwork behind her. She is particularly well acquainted with work in dairy, garden and with poultry. Her children are also at home in farm work.

RELATIVES IN U.S.A.
    None

COUNTRY PREFERRED
    U.S.A.

ELIGIBILITY FOR U.S. IMMIGRATION
    They all came to Germany in February 1945 and have been in the U.S. zone since July 1947. Mrs. Bachmann has her marriage certificate and all have their certificates of birth and baptism.

REMARKS.

Why Your Grandma Talks Funny

MENNO TRAVEL SERVICE

Christine Bachmann
Emigrated to U.S.A.

AMERICAN HEADQUARTERS
AKRON, PENNSYLVANIA

BRANCH OFFICE:
ARNOLD BOECKLINSTRASSE 11
BASEL (SWITZERLAND)

KONINGSLAAN 58 AMSTERDAM Z.
NETHERLANDS

TELEPHONE 96404
POSTGIRO 409216
CABLE ADDRESS:
MENCENCOM

November 4, 1949

Marie Brunk
Mennonite Central Committee
Stuttgart, Germany

Dear Marie:

Enclosed you will find a copy of my letter to Akron requesting payment for the Bachman family. Everything seems to be in order now and we will expect them or you to see that there is no slip up in their getting to Amsterdam.

I would appreciate being kept informed as to when they will arrive here in order to be able to meet them. You might also inform them that they will be receiving their tickets for New York on their arrival in Rotterdam. I will personally accompany them to Rotterdam and assist them through customs, etc. Should they arrive here a day earlier we will be able to put them up here at the Center. However, since at that time we are also expecting two German students who are booked for the same sailing we would appreciate greatly knowing in advance of their arrival in order that plans can be made here at the Center.

Their boat will embark between 9 and 11 a.m. on the morning of the 25th. This would mean that they should arrive at least not later than early morning of the 25th. However, it would simplify matters considerably if they could arrive the day before. This would allow for any slip-ups or snags. You should also give them my address and phone number--just in case.

Should their baggage be checked through to Amsterdam, you should definitely inform the officials that this baggage should go through directly to Amsterdam and not be held up at the German-Holland border. So much for the Bachmans! If there is anything I have failed to mention or information lacking, call or write.

Concerning the two children going to South America which we discussed at the Neustadt Conference, do you have anything further to report on them. In the meantime I have contacted the Nievelt, Gourdriaan Line in Rotterdam concerning this case. As soon as you give me the green light, I will attempt to get them passage.

Furthermore, I am in receipt of a copy of Doreen Harms' letter to you concerning Natalie Lipelt and her daughter. Should west-bound passage be desired in the course of the next two months, I should be informed soon. This would allow me to investigate the possibilities of getting them passage. Secondly, if I am informed in plenty of time it might be possible for me to get them passage on one of the cheaper boats which would be one of their concerns. From this point on, I will wait for further instructions for you before taking any action in this case.

Sincerely yours,

MENNO TRAVEL SERVICE

Paul L. Ruth

PLR:dey
cc: Doreen Harms

2......Arthur Voth:Paul Ruth

We are assuming that you are planning to meet the group on their arrival in New York. We have instructed them that they will be met in New York by someone from the Akron office.

I am very sorry that I cannot give you the exact arrival time of the ss. Leerdam. However they have informed me that it will arrive either the 6th or 7th of December.

As mentioned earlier, Mr. Kuegler's visa did not arrive in time to come to America and it was necessary to cancel this passage. Mrs. Herbert Klassen's visa also did not arrive in time which made another last minute cancellation necessary. Actually the thing that puzzles me is the fact that the office force of the Holland America Lines in Rotterdam even speaks to me anymore. However, I guess they realize how difficult it is to make any predicament when dealing with consulates, State Departments, or what have you. There is an old saying that there are three ways to do something, namely: 1. the wrong way, 2. the right way, 3. the government way. I guess the third way won out again.

We are now holding the prepaid for Mr. Kuegler in the amount of $140.00 plus $8.00 headtax for the U.S.A. and for Mrs. Klassen the prepaid amounts to $165.00 plus the $8.00 U.S. headtax. Mrs. Klassen's prepaid will be applied to another sailing for her as soon as possible. As for Mr. Kuegler, at the present time it is not exactly clear just what procedure will be followed in his case. You will probably be hearing from me in the matter of a week or so concerning Mr. Kuegler's prepaid.

For your information, I would pass on the advice that you better plan on having a fairly large vehicle meet this group in New York. The Bachman family has 9 pieces of luggage, including three very large wooden crates which are quite heavy. The two students are travelling fairly light but considering six people plus all the baggage, it will be necessary to have a fairly large vehicle.

Sincerely yours,

MENNO TRAVEL SERVICE

Paul L. Ruth

PLR:dey

dictated 26-11-49

P.S. Enclosed are also a few other statements of expenses incurred from this office for various individuals. All of these expenses are phone calls made in connection with individuals. Mr. and Mrs. Byler's expenses are phone calls made in connection with their west-bound passage. The little boy accompanying Mr. and Mrs. David Derstine to the States, Master EVRARD also has some telephone charges here which should be collected from his sponsor. I am not clear on who the sponsor is in his case but you can find that out no doubt from the Mennonite Air Section. MR. FLOYD YODER.

PLR

CRONAU:

November 2, 1949

Arthur Voth
Menno Travel Service
Akron, Pennsylvania

Dear Art:

I have now definitely booked the following passengers as listed below. Please make payment to the Holland America Line in the usual manner to the amount as listed below.

ss. Leerdam	Sailing date	Port of Embarkation	Fare
Bachman, Christine (f.)	Nov. 25	Rotterdam	$ 165.00
Bachman, Nellie (f.)	Nov. 25	Rotterdam	$ 165.00
Bachman, Mathilde (f.)	Nov. 25	Rotterdam	$ 165.00
Klassen, Mrs.	Nov. 25	Rotterdam	$ 165.00
Bachman, Artur (male)	Nov. 25	Rotterdam	$ 125.00
		Total passage fare	$ 785.00
U.S. headtax for 5 persons @ $8.00			40.00
		Total payment due	$ 825.00

To be applied against the above figure are the prepaids and part prepaids which the Holland America Line office in Rotterdam is still holding in our favor. For your information I am listing below the amounts of each prepaid and for whom the prepaid was originally held. This will make it clear just how each prepaid was applied.

Prepaids for

Mr. and Mrs. J. Penner, $160.00 each, or a total of	$ 320.00
Theo Loosli, Swiss student, $ 125.00 plus $8.00 U.S. headtax,	133.00
Delmar Wedel	125.00
Jos. Laskowski, student, prepaid was to the amount of $175.50. From this prepaid I have transferred the sum of $162.50 to Mark Layment for return passage. This leaves 13.00 credit, $5.00 for passage and $8.00 headtax	13.00
Total credit on prepaids	$ 591.00

2......Arthur Voth:Paul Ruth   2/11/49

Total due for Bachmans' passage and for Mrs. Klassen $ 825.00

Amount still held in our favor in form of prepaids at
        the Rotterdam Holland America office   591.00

        Therefore total payment to be made $ 234.00

This amount should be paid and also instruct their New York office to inform the Rotterdam office that this amount has been paid for the Bachmans' and Mrs. Klassen's passage on November 25, ss. Leerdam. This can be done by regular post as I feel there is still enough for it.

This will clear up all prepaids and parts of prepaids that are being held at the present time.

                                Sincerely yours,

                                MENNO TRAVEL SERVICE

                                Paul L. Ruth

PLR:dey

cc: Holland America Lines, Rotterdam
    MCC Menn. Aid Section
    Marie Brunk
    MTS Basel

Why Your Grandma Talks Funny

Refugee Files and Translations

Name of the Head of the Family _____

GENERAL M.C.C. QUESTIONNAIRE

A. PERSONAL DATA

Name: _____ Maiden name: _____

Date of Birth: _____ Place of Birth: (City) _____

(Country) _____

Children under 18 years (only to be entered on the "Head of Family" questionnaire):

Name	Birth Dates	Place of Birth

1 _____
2 _____
3 _____
4 _____

B. RELIGION AND PARISH

1. Which denomination do you belong to: _____
2. Are you baptized: _____ Children or adult baptism: _____
3. When: _____ Where: _____
    By whom: _____
    Why: _____
    Which church do you belong to (parish/fraternity, etc.): _____
4. If you were not accepted into the church through baptism, describe this in more detail (e.g. through marriage, handshake, letter, etc.):_____
5. When were they recorded: _____ Where: _____
    By whom: _____
6. Are both of your parents Mennonite:_____
7. Are you able to attend Mennonite devotions on Sundays: _____
    If not, what are your options:_____
    Do you attend non-Mennonite worship: _____ At which: _____
    When was the last time you attended regular Mennonite services: _____ Where: _____
8. Are you a member or supporter of any other religious community: (e.g., Jehovah's Witnesses, Adventists, etc.) _____ Which:_____

C. OCCUPATIONAL AND HEALTH

1. How many years of schooling did you have:_____
   Where: (Country)_____
2. Learned occupation:_____Second job: _____
3. Full-time employment before 1940:_____
   Today's employment:_____
4. How much do you earn monthly: _____
5. What did you live on after the collapse and before the currency reform:
   _____
6. Are you satisfied with your apartment by today's standards: _____
7. Are you physically healthy:_____If not, describe your suffering or infirmity: _____
8. Are your children under 18 healthy (only for the head of the family):
   If not, describe their suffering: _____

D. EMIGRATION

1. Would you like to emigrate at any cost:_____ Which is the main reason: _____

   Different reasons: _____
2. In which country (first choice): _____

   Second choice:_____
3. If to Canada:
   a) Do you have a guarantor:_____How are you related: _____
   b) Name and address of the guarantor: _____
   c) Your identification number is:_____
   d) Are you before the I.R.O been commission:_____
      When:_____Where: _____
      What was the result: (Accepted/rejected) _____
   e) If already appeared before the Canadian office, why were they cancelled: _____
      When: _____
      Deferred: _____
      When: _____ For how long: _____
4. If to South America, in which country: (Paraguay/Uruguay)_____

If there is a basic relationship, please indicate degree of relationship: _____
   Other special reasons:(stepping stone to Canada, etc.) _____

Refugee Files and Translations

5. If to U.S.A., for what reasons: _____

E. VARIOUS

1. Are you married/widowed:_____ With whom: _____
   Name before marriage: _____

2. Are you divorced:_____ In which year:_____ By whom: _____

3. Are they civil and/or church weddings: _____

4. Do you have illegitimate children:_____ How many:_____
   Name of the father: _____

5. Are you engaged:_____ Is fiancé Mennonite:_____
   Imperial German:_____

6. Are you ready—if necessary—to emigrate without him/her: _____

7. Is your husband/wife missing:_____ Since when: _____
   What message do you have:_____

8. Were you in the Armed Forces:_____ If so, by:_____ To:_____
   Were you in the SS:_____ If so, by:_____ To:_____
   What physical traces are left behind:_____

9. Were you a member of the Communist party/godless union: _____
   Were you a member of the NSDAP or one of its branches: _____
   If so, inform about the denazification: Level 1, 2, 3, 4, 5, — not affected

10. When did you come to Germany:_____ Country of origin: _____

11. Citizenship before 1939: _____

12. Were you naturalized in the German Empire:_____ When: _____
    Where:_____
    Did the naturalization take place on request or on command: _____
    If on command, describe details: _____

13. Were you settled in Poland:_____

14. Do you have relatives in Russian ban:_____ How many:_____
    Name and address of relatives in Russia (for the purpose of possible MCC work in Russia):_____

15. Do you receive old-age benefits, widows or orphan's pension:_____
    If so, how much per month:_____

16. If necessary, can you come to Gronau for a few days without the help of MCC: _____

17. Name relatives, no matter how extensive, among the refugees in Germany

Why Your Grandma Talks Funny

(VERY IMPORTANT), including last name, first name, date of birth, kinship, and address in Germany

a) _____
b) _____
c) _____
d) _____
e) _____
f) _____
g) _____
h) _____

Full Address:

_____ Date: _____

_____ Signature: _____

_____

ONLY FOR MCC

a) Reference Letter:

b) Personal Interview: